D0888995

RSA00002

ISBN# 09679546-2-2

Cellular Health Series:

Cancer

Matthias Rath, M.D.

First Edition, February 2002

"We will live to see a time when we no longer have to look over our shoulder like a criminal when we say: two and two makes four."

Bertolt Brecht, "Life of Galilee"

Contents

Principles of Natural Therapies

- Vitamin C and Lysine—Key Molecules of Cellular Health
- Collagen Production—a Key to Disease Prevention and Control
- Nutritional Supplementation with Proline, Lysine, and Vitamin C
- How Much Vitamin C?—A Tolerance Test

Questions and Answers

Literature and Sources

Introduction

Foreword

This book provides a summary of the progress of Cellular Health in the battle against several forms of cancer and infectious diseases, as well as other serious diseases. It substantiates the fact that cancer—after heart disease, the second-largest plague of mankind—will lose its threat. This book discloses key mechanisms, describing how cancer cells spread through the body and how this process can be blocked in a natural way. All this can be done without chemotherapy, radiation therapy, and other dangerous and ineffective approaches used today by conventional medicine. It is no surprise, therefore, that the Cellular Health approach can help in diseases that conventional medicine still considers incurable.

The scientific foundation of this discovery and the information about its applications has been available since 1992, through my personal scientific investigations and publications. From a historical perspective, this scientific breakthrough in Cellular Health in the fields of cancer and infectious diseases must be noted as an example of medical science—capable of saving millions of lives—being suppressed for the sake of the pharmaceutical industry and other special-interest groups, who make profits from the existence of diseases.

One of the methods with which the pharmaceutical industry, tries to secure its worldwide power is to ignore the simple and logical causes of common diseases. By using the Latin language and complicated diagnostic medical terminology, millions of patients have been kept in the dark, handing over the responsibility for their own bodies and health to the medical pharma-cartel. This has suddenly changed with the discovery that heart infarctions and strokes are nothing else but early stages of the sailors' disease scurvy, and they are possible to cure with Vitamin C and other nutrients. The rationale behind the origin of heart disease has been explained in my book "Cellular Health Series-The Heart", in a way that can be understood even by a child.

This simple but important discovery shook the world as it was shaken once before, 400 years ago. In those days the discovery that the Earth revolved around the Sun instead of the other way around shook the foundations of those in power. In our time, it is the discovery that heart disease is not a disease but the result of a chronic vitamin deficiency and thus preventable. Practical implementation of this discovery will undermine a multi-million-dollar market of questionable pharmaceutical drugs. Even more, it removes a smoke screen placed on the origin of such common disease as heart disease. With the understanding of the causes of diseases, patients today have become responsible citizens who can take their health interests into their own hands.

The book you are holding in your hands will also remove the screen that was placed in front of cancer. The knowledge of this disease presented in this book is so logical and understandable that it will soon become an integral part of health education in schools. New natural cancer therapies will also terminate the lucrative pharmaceutical business of destructive chemotherapeutics.

If you find the information in this book helpful to you, do not keep it to yourself. Make use of it! I invite you to help building a new health-care system that will finally serve the health interests of the people and not share in the profit-making practices of the pharmaceutical industry.

Do this for yourself and out of responsibility for your children's generation!

Yours truly,

Matthias Rath, M.D.

The End of Common Diseases

This picture presents the latest available statistics of the World Health Organization regarding the main causes of death in Europe, the United States, and other industrialized countries at the end of the twentieth century.

Every year 12 million people worldwide die of the results of atherosclerosis, heart infarctions, and strokes. These are by far the most common causes of death of our time. Cellular Medicine has already found an answer to this epidemic: atherosclerosis and its consequences, heart infarction and stroke are early forms of scurvy. Based on this knowledge, coronary heart disease will be reduced to a fraction of the current figures over the next decades.

The second-largest common disease is cancer—malignant tumors. Coronary disease and cancer together are responsible for over 80% of all deaths in industrialized countries. Incidences of cancer keep increasing on a global scale. There is only one plausible explanation for this: conventional medicine does not know the causes for cancer nor how this disease spreads. Because of this there is no effective cancer therapy available and the disease can keep expanding on a global scale.

The most common diseases and causes of death in developing countries are infectious diseases, including the AIDS epidemic. These serious infectious diseases can only continue spreading the way they do because the knowledge of cellular health has been not efficiently used. This book will also provide the solution for the control of these diseases.

Common Diseases and Causes of Death

- World Health Organization 1997-

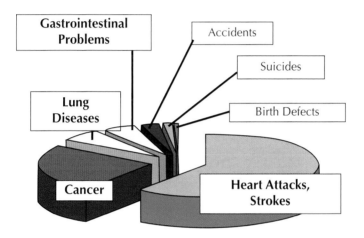

Gastrointestinal Problems

Accidents

Suicides

Lung Diseases

Birth Defects

Cancer

Heart Attacks, Strokes

Eight out of ten people die of
coronary heart disease or cancer

The Fundamental Question of Cellular Health: Where Does the Problem Originate in a Cell?

Basically, the origin of disease can be considered from two cellular aspects: the lack of biological fuel needed by the cell's power plants, the mitochondria, or a failure in the function of the nucleus, the metabolic control center of the cell.

1. Lack of biological fuel in the power plants of the cell (mitochondria). Coronary heart disease, for instance, is mainly caused by an insufficient supply to the cell of biological fuel in the form of vitamins and other cell factors. These nutrients are needed for the conversion of food into cellular energy, which is used by the cell in many metabolic reactions. Another example is heart failure, which is caused by a lack of bio-fuel in the cells of the heart muscle. With low energy production the pumping function of the heart muscle becomes impaired, causing shortness of breath and the accumulation of fluids in the body. Generally the supply of vitamins and other bio-energy fuel will correct the impaired pumping function of the heart muscle.

2. Diseases caused by a problem in the cell's metabolic program. The second largest cause of diseases in general is an error in the metabolic software of the cell's control center, the nucleus. Like a computer virus that will disrupt a computer's normal functions, cells can fall under the control of a disease program. The most important diseases in this group are infectious diseases (such as virus infections) and cancer.

This faulty programming will lead to a disease only when two preconditions have been met:

a) programming error causes uncontrolled "cell multiplication," and at the same time

b) programming error causes a "disruption of the organization of the surrounding connective tissue," which enables the diseased cells to spread.

The mechanisms that facilitate the spread of these aggressive diseases and the possibilities of slowing down or stopping their progress will be discussed later in detail.

Diseases Originate
Inside the Cells

Most common cause of disease:
Lack of Biological Fuel in the Cell Power Plant

A lack of bio-energy carriers
(vitamins, minerals, trace elements) in the powerplants of
the cell (mitochondria)

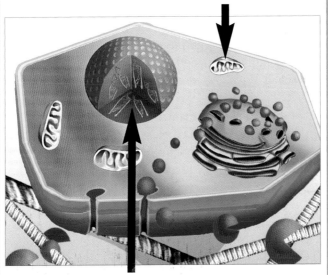

Second most common cause of disease:
Reprogramming of the cell's
control system

Aggressive diseases, such as virus infections and cancer,
can spread by the reprogramming of the metabolic
control system within the cell's nucleus.

How Cells Move Through the Body

If we want to understand how disease spreads in the body, we have to take a look at the way cells move through the body. This is easy to explain in the case of red and white blood cells: these cells are just carried along in the blood stream. However, it is more difficult to imagine how cells composing other organs can move through a body's strong connective tissue. This happens every second inside our bodies.

In order to move through the connective tissue, any cell has to be capable of temporarily dissolving the surrounding tissue—the collagen and elastic fibers -so it can make its way through. For this purpose the cells use enzymes that can temporarily digest and weaken the connective fibers surrounding them. All enzymes are proteins, which are produced by the cells themselves and then secreted. In order to become active, many enzymes bind to other specific molecules, such as trace elements, which change their biochemical structure and induce their activity. Cellular migration through dense tissue requires that the cell secrete enzymes that can dissolve the surrounding collagen. This is why these protein molecules are known as collagen-digesting enzymes.

In addition, the cell often needs to secrete activators— the molecules that can vitalize dormant enzymes located outside the cell,enabling them to digest and loosen up the surrounding collagen molecules.

For easy understanding, we show collagen-dissolving enzymes with red, circled "choppers". Further scientific details regarding the pathway of enzymatic activation stages can be found in the Question and Answer chapter at the end of the book.

Cell Movements Through Body Tissue

Cell nucleus initiates the production of enzymes that dissolve collagen

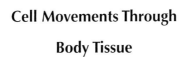

A

Production of these enzymes in the cell

Secretion of enzymes into the surrounding tissue

Enzyme molecules making their way through collagen fibers of the tissue

B

Tissue around the cell is *temporarily* dissolved

Cell can move through body tissue

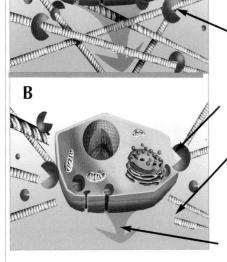

15

Collagen-Dissolving Cell Systems

Most cells of the body are capable of producing enzymes that can "eat" their way through connective tissue. In healthy people this takes place in certain, biologically defined physiological stages. In a disease, this happens when cells and cellular systems become reprogrammed. Cancer cells, for instance, use these "biological weapons" to multiply inside an organ and then spread through the entire body (metastasis). Viruses and other microorganisms also use this collagen-dissolving "weapon" to spread an infection to other parts of the body.

How is it possible that a single disease mechanism—the destruction of collagen by protein-digesting enzymes—is of such extraordinary value that it plays a vital role in all serious diseases? The body itself uses the same mechanism in a healthy person for its normal functions, in various metabolic pathways or to restructure certain organs. For instance, enzymatic degradation of the connective tissue is important in the function of the body's immune system, during growth, and also in the restructuring of the reproductive organs during the monthly female cycle and in pregnancy.

However, our bodies are completely helpless when the mechanism that it normally uses becomes activated and abused, such as by invading microbes. As soon as the virus or cancer cell is capable of overcoming the body with its own collagen-dissolving weapons, the disease starts spreading aggressively.

To explain this fundamental principle that distinguishes our health from disease, we will look at how the body uses this collagen-dissolving mechanism to perform its normal physiological functions.

Cell Systems that Use a Collagen Dissolving Mechanism

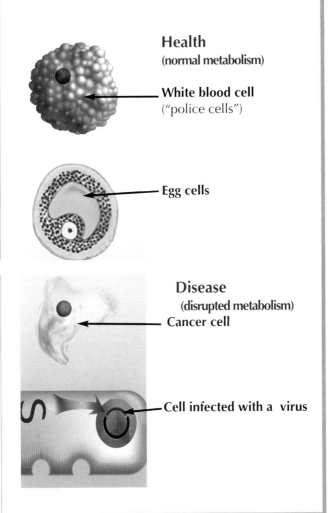

Health
(normal metabolism)

White blood cell
("police cells")

Egg cells

Disease
(disrupted metabolism)

Cancer cell

Cell infected with a virus

Notes

Restructuring of Collagen in Healthy People

- **Protection Against Infections**

- **Ovulation**

Protection against Infections

The body's basic protection against invaders (microbes) is secured by the white blood cells ("police cells"). There are several subgroups of white blood cells that perform specific functions in the immune system. Especially important are the macrophages, which can "eat" and digest invaders. Immature forms of these "eating cells," called monocytes, can reach every part of the body through the blood stream. If an infection takes place in a part of the body such as in the lungs, the body releases "alarm substances" that attract monocytes to the source of microbial invasion.

The police cells arriving through the blood stream then have to traverse the blood vessel wall and move into the lung tissue with the help of collagen-digesting enzymes. Using this mechanism in the blood capillary wall, the police cells can temporarily create a little space between the cells in the blood vessel wall (endothelium), which allow them to move from the blood into the lung tissue.

To reach the site in the lungs that has been invaded by viruses and bacteria, the eating cells must be able to move through the lung tissue. In order to do this, monocytes use the same collagen-dissolving mechanism. They secrete collagen-digesting enzymes in the direction of the infection. This way cells can loosen up the dense connective surrounding tissue and move through the tissue much like an expedition that cuts its way through the jungle with a machete.

The connective tissue will close again right after the cell has passed through, using the compensating mechanisms that repair the tissue. This repair is assured by the optimal production of collagen molecules that require a sufficient supply of vitamin C and other cell factors in the diet.

Collagen Dissolving in the Immune System

- Example: Lung Infection -

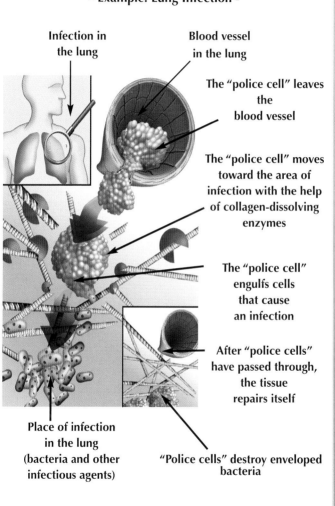

Infection in the lung

Blood vessel in the lung

The "police cell" leaves the blood vessel

The "police cell" moves toward the area of infection with the help of collagen-dissolving enzymes

The "police cell" engulfs cells that cause an infection

After "police cells" have passed through, the tissue repairs itself

Place of infection in the lung (bacteria and other infectious agents)

"Police cells" destroy enveloped bacteria

Ovulation

One of the most fascinating functions in which the body continuously uses a collagen-dissolving mechanism is the ovulation process in the female body. Monthly hormonal changes in the first half of the female cycle stimulate certain cell types (granulocytes), which build the wall around the ripening egg cell (follicle). These cells produce large amounts of fluid rich in collagen-digesting enzymes.

In the middle of the cycle, the ripened egg contains so much collagen-digesting enzyme that it is capable of temporarily disrupting the collagen tissue of the ovarian wall. This mechanism operates every month, allowing the egg cell to move from the ovary through the fallopian tube and into the womb (uterus).

It is understandable that this mechanism needs to be precisely timed and to be confined to a specific location. This mechanism must assure that only one egg per cycle ripens and passes through. Therefore, it is absolutely necessary that collagen-digesting enzymes remain in a timely and physiological balance with the mechanism that blocks these enzymes and initiates self-healing of the tissue.

Immediately after the egg cell has left the ovary, the activity of collagen-digesting enzymes is blocked by the body's own enzymatic blocks. This shifts the balance toward collagen-producing mechanisms, which dominate over the collagen-destroying process. Using this mechanism the tissue of the ovary wall can quickly heal and close itself. Four weeks later, during the next cycle, the whole process repeats itself, taking place in the body of every healthy woman until menopause.

Collagen Dissolving During Ovulation

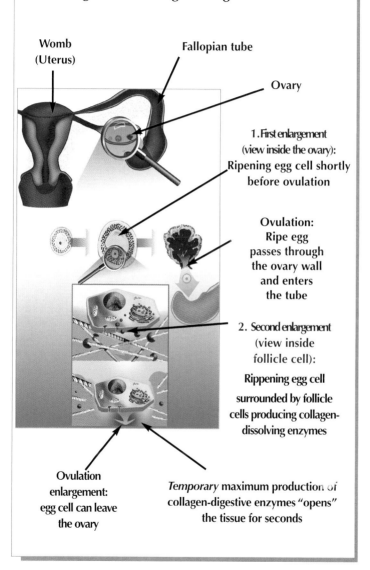

Womb
(Uterus)

Fallopian tube

Ovary

1. First enlargement
(view inside the ovary):
Ripening egg cell shortly
before ovulation

Ovulation:
Ripe egg
passes through
the ovary wall
and enters
the tube

2. Second enlargement
(view inside
follicle cell):

Rippening egg cell
surrounded by follicle
cells producing collagen-
dissolving enzymes

Ovulation
enlargement:
egg cell can leave
the ovary

Temporary maximum production of
collagen-digestive enzymes "opens"
the tissue for seconds

Notes

Degradation of Collagen
Is a Precondition for
the Spread of Diseases

- Collagen Dissolving in Infectious Diseases

- Collagen Dissolving in Cancer

- How Cancer Spreads—Metastasis

- Collagen Dissolving in Chronic Inflammation

- Collagen Dissolving inAdvanced Atherosclerosis

Collagen Dissolving in Infectious Diseases

The collagen-dissolving mechanism plays an especially important role in infectious diseases. Without the disruption of the surrounding connective tissue, the agents that cause diseases (viruses, bacteria) cannot invade the body and spread the disease. The illustration on the next page shows how this mechanism is used in the development of an influenza infection.

Unlike all other cells, which contain both metabolic software (in the nucleus) and hardware (production system for protein and other metabolic molecules), a virus consists only of software (genetic information). If it wants to reproduce it has to multiply inside a host cell using the host's cell hardware. In the case of a flu virus, the host cell can be a cell of the mucous membrane in the nose, throat, or lungs. As soon as the virus has invaded the host cell, it incorporates its genetic information into the nucleus of the host. This allows the virus to convert metabolic functions of the host cell for its own purposes and spread the infection through:

1. Multiplication of the virus. The metabolic production system of the host cell receives an order to multiply the virus particles. After multiple reproduction cycles, virus particles are released by the host cell into the surrounding area where the newly made viruses can invade new cells.

2. Mass production of collagen-dissolving enzymes. The virus also orders the host cell to produce collagen-digesting enzymes. The host cell excretes these enzymes, which start to dissolve the surrounding tissue. The infection then can easily spread to other parts of the body.

   The more a virus is capable of using the metabolism of a host cell for these two purposes, the faster a virus infection will spread and the sicker a patient will feel.

Collagen Dissolving
in Virus Infections (e.g., the Flu)

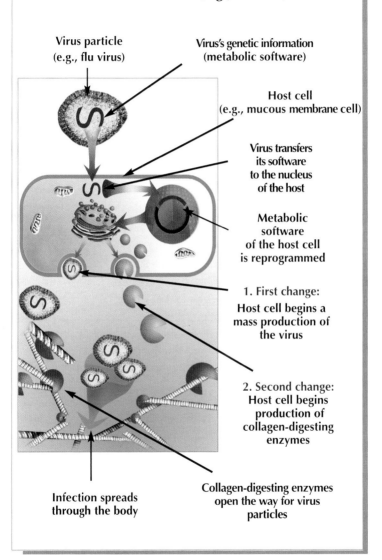

Virus particle
(e.g., flu virus)

Virus's genetic information
(metabolic software)

Host cell
(e.g., mucous membrane cell)

Virus transfers
its software
to the nucleus
of the host

Metabolic
software
of the host cell
is reprogrammed

1. First change:
Host cell begins a
mass production of
the virus

2. Second change:
Host cell begins
production of
collagen-digesting
enzymes

Collagen-digesting enzymes
open the way for virus
particles

Infection spreads
through the body

Collagen Dissolving in Cancer

All forms of cancer spread with the help of the tissue-dissolving mechanism. This illustration shows an example of the development of liver cancer.

The liver is the body's central metabolic organ, and it is responsible for neutralizing and removing toxins from the body. The toxins entering the body from the diet, such as pesticides and preservatives, are the most common cause of liver cancer. Also, all pharmaceutical drugs have to be detoxified in the liver. In this context, in January 1996, the Journal of the American Medical Association (JAMA) issued a warning that all cholesterol-lowering medications (statins) used on the market at that time were carcinogenic (cancer causing).

Liver cells that are exposed to these poisonous substances can either be destroyed or permanently damaged. This damage often involves an error in the genetic program of the cells (cell's software), similar to what we have seen in virus infections. This damage can trigger two processes that facilitate the development of cancer:

1. Uncontrolled cell multiplication. The software of a cancer cell is reprogrammed in such a way that it causes constant reproduction and multiplication of the cell. This uncontrolled cellular multiplication is the first precondition for cancer to develop.

2. Mass production of collagen-digesting enzymes. The second precondition is the production of enzymes that destroy the surrounding connective tissue that would otherwise keep the cancer cells confined.

Research has established that the more enzymes a cancer cell produces, the more aggressively the cancer develops. The faster the cancer can spread through a body, the shorter the life expectancy of the patient if the mechanism is not stopped.

Collagen Dissolving in Cancer

- Local Growth of Cancer -

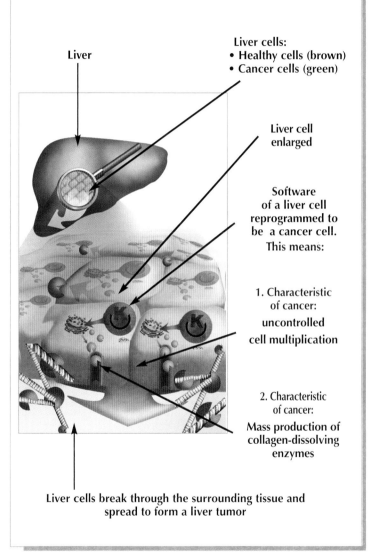

Liver

Liver cells:
• Healthy cells (brown)
• Cancer cells (green)

Liver cell
enlarged

Software
of a liver cell
reprogrammed to
be a cancer cell.
This means:

1. Characteristic
of cancer:
uncontrolled
cell multiplication

2. Characteristic
of cancer:
Mass production of
collagen-dissolving
enzymes

Liver cells break through the surrounding tissue and
spread to form a liver tumor

How Cancer Spreads (Metastasis)

The collagen-dissolving mechanism also plays a major role in the spread of cancer and the growth of secondary tumors in other organs or parts of the body (metastasis). The illustration shows the metastasis of a liver tumor.

Small blood vessels provide oxygen and nutrients to tumor cells. The walls of these blood capillaries are not obstacles for a cancer cell. With the help of collagen-digesting enzymes, a cancer cell can "eat" its way into the lumen of the small blood vessel and into the blood stream. The blood can then carry away cancer cells, by which they can spread and invade other organs.

In this example, the obstacles for the cancer cell in the blood stream are small lung capillaries that supply oxygen to the blood. The diameter of these capillaries is smaller than a hair, so the cancer cell attaches itself to the wall of the capillary and "eats" its way in with the help of collagen-dissolving enzymes. This way the cell can enter the lung tissue. In the lung, the cancer cell starts to multiply and develop into a secondary tumor, the metastasis. Inside the lung the same kind of tumor will now grow as the original one did in the liver.

The same rule applies to the development of secondary tumors: the more collagen-digesting enzymes a specific cancer cell can produce, the faster secondary tumors will develop—not only in the lungs but also in other organs—and the more ill a patient will become.

Collagen Dissolving in Cancer

- Cancer Spreading Through the Body -

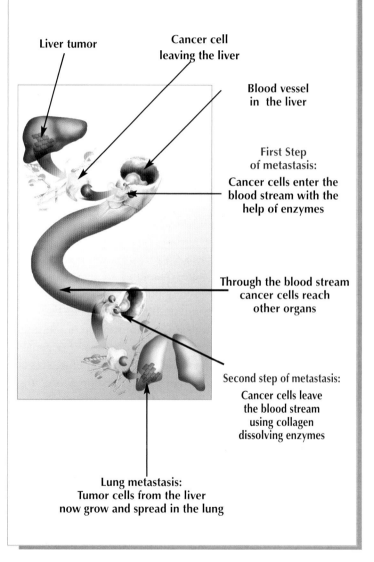

Liver tumor

Cancer cell
leaving the liver

Blood vessel
in the liver

First Step
of metastasis:
Cancer cells enter the
blood stream with the
help of enzymes

Through the blood stream
cancer cells reach
other organs

Second step of metastasis:
Cancer cells leave
the blood stream
using collagen
dissolving enzymes

Lung metastasis:
Tumor cells from the liver
now grow and spread in the lung

Collagen Dissolving in Chronic Inflammation

Collagen-digesting enzymes also play a crucial part in the spread of other diseases. The picture shows an example of a long-term inflammation of the knee joint (chronic arthritis).

The body's defense cells play a crucial role in the fight against inflammation. As you already know, the defense cells belong to the group of white blood cells (leukocytes). Because of their function, these cells are often called the "police cells." Especially important in this group in the battle against "foreign" substances and also in the "clearance of the inflammation battlefield" are the so-called "eating-cells" (macrophages).

What happens if an inflammation continues for a long time because the invaders' attack is too powerful and the body engages too many of its police cells? The result is that the eating cells secrete high quantities of their "defense substances" over a long period of time. This defense weapon consists not only of collagen-digesting enzymes but also of a load of free radicals. As we saw in the example of the lung infection, the police cells use collagen-destroying enzymes to move through thick connective tissue to get to the area of infection. If the immune system's battle on the site of the inflammation takes too long, then huge amounts of collagen-dissolving enzymes are secreted, creating a problem: the inflammation will erode the surrounding connective tissue and turn into a chronic (long-term) process.

Chronic inflammations are not simply restricted to bone joints but can also be found in all organs of the body. However, independent of the organ where the inflammation takes place, the body will always use the same defense cells and mechanisms.

Collagen Dissolving in
Chronic Inflammation
- e.g., Inflammation of the Joint (Arthritis) -

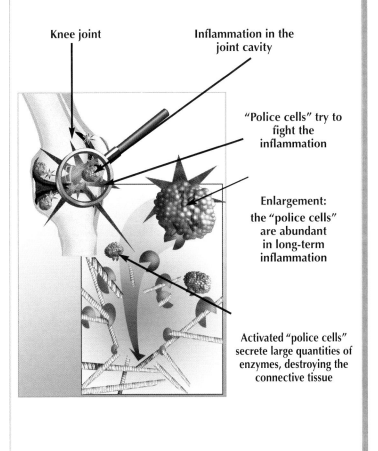

Knee joint

Inflammation in the joint cavity

"Police cells" try to fight the inflammation

Enlargement:
the "police cells" are abundant in long-term inflammation

Activated "police cells" secrete large quantities of enzymes, destroying the connective tissue

Over secretion of collagen dissolving enzymes contributes to the continuation of the disease. An *acute* inflammation turns to a *chronic* one.

33

Collagen Dissolving
in Advanced Atherosclerosis

During the growth of atherosclerotic plaques (deposits), even in advanced stages of atherosclerosis, the process of collagen destruction plays an important role.

It is generally known that, as in the sailors' disease scurvy, the initial step in the development of atherosclerosis is a lack of vitamins in the arterial wall. As a result of this vitamin deficiency the arteries of the heart weaken, which triggers a repair process to stabilize the wall of these blood vessels. Initially, the body mobilizes fatty particles (lipoproteins) and other repair molecules from the blood to deposit them in the weakest areas of the arterial wall.

When these repair measures become inadequate the weakening arterial wall is further stabilized through an uncontrolled growth of the cells that build the vascular wall. These cells, called smooth-muscle cells, migrate from the outermost cell layer of the artery to the area that contains atherosclerotic fatty deposits. These muscle cells have to move through a very strong and dense intermediate layer of collagen fibers and connective tissue—the basal membrane. In order to do that, smooth-muscle cells produce collagen-digesting enzymes that can loosen-up the collagen and let them pass through the basal membrane and move in the direction of the plaque.

Naturally, the effective approach in the prevention and treatment of atherosclerosis is to preserve the integrity of the artery walls, which can be achieved through an optimal supply of vitamins.

In the next part of this book we will discuss the mechanisms that can block the disintegration of collagen in a natural way.

Collagen Dissolving in
Advanced Atherosclerosis

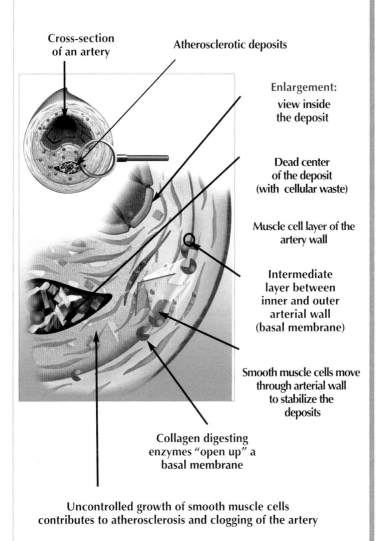

Cross-section of an artery

Atherosclerotic deposits

Enlargement:
view inside the deposit

Dead center of the deposit (with cellular waste)

Muscle cell layer of the artery wall

Intermediate layer between inner and outer arterial wall (basal membrane)

Smooth muscle cells move through arterial wall to stabilize the deposits

Collagen digesting enzymes "open up" a basal membrane

Uncontrolled growth of smooth muscle cells contributes to atherosclerosis and clogging of the artery

Notes

Natural Prevention of Collagen Degradation and Enzyme-Blocking Therapy

- Lysine as a Natural Enzyme Block
- The Remarkable Value of Lysine
- The Balance between Collagen-Dissolving Enzymes and Lysine
- Successful Use of Enzyme Blocks in Cancer Therapy
- The Use of Lysine in Other Serious Diseases
- Conventional Cancer Therapy —a Dead-End Street
- Cancer — No Longer a Death Warrant
- Blocks and AIDS

Lysine as a Natural Enzyme Block

In the previous chapters we have learned about the role of collagen dissolving in facilitating the spread of diseases through the body. The activation of this collagen-dissolving mechanism leads to the development of aggressive diseases such as cancer and microbial infections. Apart from that, this mechanism plays an important role in all diseases that progress to advanced stages. Every therapeutic possibility that will halt this mechanism or even slow it down will therefore be one of the most important successes in the field of medicine.

Nature itself provides us with two large groups of molecules that can block collagen digestion and its dissolving actions. The first group is the body's intrinsic enzymatic block that can stop the action of collagen-digesting enzymes in a few moments. The second group is the enzyme-blocking substances that come from our diet or as dietary supplement. The most important one in this group is the natural amino acid L-lysine. When lysine is supplied in a sufficient amount as a dietary supplement, it can block the anchor sites in the connective tissue that collagen-digesting enzymes use to attach themselves to the tissue. In this way lysine prevents these enzymes from uncontrollably disintegrating connective tissue.

This is illustrated on the next page: while the cells still produce high levels of collagen-digesting enzymes, in the presence of lysine these enzymes are no longer effective in breaking down collagen. Therefore, uncontrolled destruction of collagen and connective-tissue structure can be prevented. This way the spread of diseases can be slowed down or stopped.

Lysine Is the Most Effective Natural Way to Block Collagen-Digesting Enzymes

Lysine, the natural enzyme block must be supplied from the diet

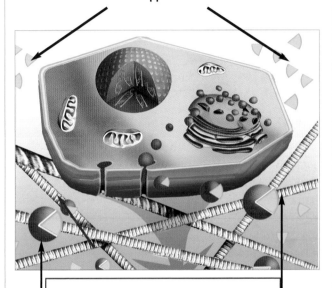

Lysine occupies the areas
where enzymes bind to the tissue
(anchor sites) andblocks their effects

Collagen-dissolving
enzyme

Prevention of uncontrolled
collagen destruction

The Remarkable Value of Lysine

All metabolic functions in the human body are controlled by biological language. To date, some twenty known amino acids compose all the proteins in our bodies. These building blocks of life function like the letters of the alphabet. Our body uses various combinations of amino acids to create innumerable biological words (peptides) and sentences (proteins). Separate amino acids (letters) also have important "individual" metabolic functions, and lysine is a prime example.

The cells of the body can produce most amino acids themselves. These amino acids are called nonessential. However, there are nine known amino acids that our body cannot produce, and they have to be supplied through the diet. These amino acids are called essential (needed for life).

Within the group of essential amino acids, lysine plays a similarly important role as vitamin C does within the vitamin group. The daily requirement of lysine surpasses that of all other amino acids. Among its many functions, lysine is also the basic building block of the amino acid carnitine, which is important for energy metabolism in every cell.

The fact that the human body can store a large amount of this amino acid is proof enough of its importance for our health. About 25% of collagen, the most abundant and important structural molecule of bones, skin, blood vessel walls, and all other organs, consists of two amino acids, lysine and proline. As the summary on the next page shows, a person weighing 70 kg (155 lb.) has about 500 g (1.1 lb.) of lysine stored in the body at all times.

Taking large quantities of lysine will not cause adverse effects. Our metabolism is familiar with handling large amounts of lysine, and it will simply excrete the molecules that are not used. Rather, the opposite is generally the case: Almost all people suffer from a chronic deficiency of lysine.

Lysine Molecule—Made by Nature

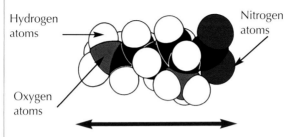

Hydrogen atoms

Nitrogen atoms

Oxygen atoms

**1 nm = 1 Millionth of a Millimeter
(10,000 times smaller than a body cell)**

How much lysine can our bodies handle?

- A human body weighing about 155 lbs contains about 22 lbs of proteins.

- 50% of this protein mass is present as the connective tissue proteins, collagen and elastin

- The amino acid lysine forms about 12% of the collagen and elastin mass, which means about 1.1 lb to 1.3 lbs.

- A human body weighing 155 lb. therefore contains about 1.1 lb. of lysine.

Since our bodies are accustomed to such large amounts of lysine, taking 4 oz. or 8 oz. of lysine daily as a dietary supplement should not be considered as excessive.

The Balance between Collagen-Dissolving Enzymes and Lysine

We have already learned that enzyme activity can be blocked with the body's own molecules and with those supplied through the diet, such as lysine. The body's own block (enzymatic inhibitor) is the first line of defense that assures the balance among the body's systems and keeps them in check. In the illustration, the enzyme block produced by the body is represented by green arrows. Lysine molecules have the same function but are the second line of defense, ready to step in when the body's own systems are insufficient. The lysine block cannot overshoot its goal, even when taken in high amounts, such as 4 oz. or 8 oz. a day.

A second important fact shown in the illustration is the balance between the collagen-dissolving mechanism (red) and its blocking mechanism (green) during sickness and health. In normal conditions these systems are in perfect balance. When "police cells" are wandering through the body, the balance is disturbed. But the healthy body then restores the balance within moments.

In cancer and other previously described diseases, this balance becomes disrupted in favor of the collagen-dissolving mechanism. Because the natural cellular mechanisms cannot sufficiently block the collagen-disintegration process, a high-dosage dietary supplement of lysine is the only possible therapy to stop or to slow down this process. The goal of this therapy is to correct the disrupted balance with a long-term high concentration of lysine to block disintegration.

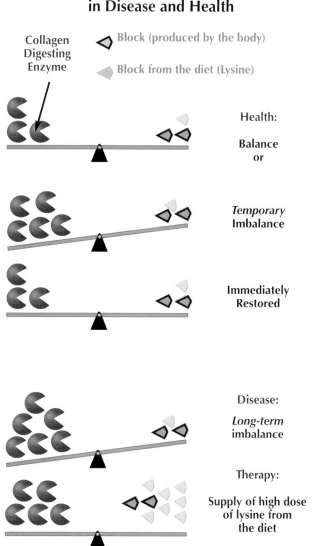

Collagen Digesting Enzymes
and Their Blocks
in Disease and Health

Collagen
Digesting
Enzyme

Block (produced by the body)

Block from the diet (Lysine)

Health:

Balance
or

Temporary
Imbalance

Immediately
Restored

Disease:

Long-term
imbalance

Therapy:

Supply of high dose
of lysine from
the diet

43

Successful Use of Enzyme Blocks in Cancer Therapy

Efficient control of the spread of a disease by collagen-dissolving enzyme blocks has been successful with several diseases. This is especially important in diseases for which orthodox medicine has no preventive or healing therapies yet. This includes the forms of cancer illustrated on the next page.

To date hundreds of studies have established that a high-dosage supply of vitamin C, vitamin E, beta-carotene, and other dietary supplements can prevent several forms of cancer. There is more information on this subject in the literature listed in the bibliography. A supply of vitamins in high dosages forms the basis for every current cancer therapy. Vitamin therapy has achieved therapeutic success in hormone-independent forms of cancer, whereas in hormone-dependent forms of cancer the natural therapies have been either hardly effective or not successful.

Now, for the first time we have at our disposal an effective form of a natural therapy, based on blocking the enzymatic destruction of collagen. As seen in the example of ovulation, these collagen-dissolving enzymes are in particular activated by hormones; therefore the use of lysine in high dosages can be effective in treating all forms of cancer. In 1977, a Swedish research group led by Dr. Astedt from the University of Lund reported the successful treatment of breast cancer with enzyme blocks:

Secondary tumours were already developing in the brain of the patient with breast cancer. Radiation and chemotherapy were without results. While under the treatment with enzymatic blocks the brain metastasis and other symptoms of the illness began to diminish. One year after the treatment the patient was free of complaints.

Enzyme-blocking Therapy for Cancer

Hormone-*dependent* forms of cancer	Hormone-*independent* forms of cancer

**Breast cancer
(Mammary Carcinoma)**

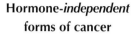

Stomach cancer

**Cancer of the womb
(Uterine Carcinoma)**

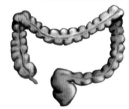

Colon cancer

**Cancer of the ovary
(Ovarian Carcinoma)**

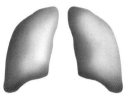

Lung cancer

Skin cancer

This patient was treated with tranexamic acid, a synthetic derivative of the natural amino acid lysine. This chemically modified form of lysine is many times stronger than the natural substance; it is artificial and can be used by prescription only. High dosages of lysine will have a similar result but without the side effects associated with the use of tranexamic acid.

In the Journal of the American Medical Association (JAMA), July 11, 1977, the same research group presented spectacular successes in the treatment of ovarian tumors. Even in very advanced cases—with secondary tumors in other organs—the enzyme-blocking therapy led to the encapsulation of the tumors, stopping them from spreading further.

In 1980, a group of scientists from the University of Tokyo led by Dr. Suma published the following:

The treatment was successful in a patient with advanced, inoperable ovarian cancer. The disease had already caused secondary tumors and fluid accumulation in the stomach. Even in this advanced stage the cancer was brought to a standstill with the help of enzyme block therapy. The researchers had observed the development of the disease for several years and closed the case as follows: "Three years after the start of the treatment the patient had no more complaints."

By far the most common form of cancer in women is breast cancer, followed by uterine and ovarian cancers. The physiology of the breast tissue and its hormonal restructuring during the monthly cycle makes it particularly prone to cancerous transformations. If there is some kind of disturbance in the regulatory mechanisms, the tissue slips toward steady restructuring, which eventually can lead to uncontrolled growth of tissue and the formation of tumors.

Considering the fact that in Europe alone hundreds of thousands of women die of this form of cancer every year, the question poses itself: Why does it take so long before safe and potentially successful forms of therapy, such as enzyme-blocking therapy, are generally applied? The answer is simple: Cancer and chemotherapeutic drugs are the second-most lucrative market for the pharmaceutical industry after the heart disease market. The global market for chemotherapeutics alone makes a profit of over a hundred billion dollars a year. This is why the pharmaceutical industry has no interest in the development of therapies that could put an end to cancer.

Even in the few cases when the blocking of collagen-digesting enzymes was studied, only synthetic derivatives of lysine were used. The reason is also economical: contrary to the natural lysine, its chemically modified forms could be patented and therefore be profitable for the pharmaceutical business. A wider use of even these patented substances could also mean the end of cancer.

For years the first successful reports on this new therapy have been ignored by the pharmaceutical industry. It was only in 1992, with the publication of my scientific research, that the meaning of this medical breakthrough and the therapeutic use of lysine in all fields of medicine became known.

The Use of Lysine in Other Serious Diseases

The therapeutic applications for lysine in the fight against disease are not restricted to cancer. It can be used in the natural treatment of many other diseases for which orthodox medicine has not yet found a solution. Diseases that can be treated with high dosages of lysine are listed in the table on the next page.

In atherosclerosis, lysine can help stop the spread and growth of deposits (atherosclerotic plaques) in the arteries of the heart and brain. At the same time, with the help of vitamins and other dietary supplements, a natural healing process of the arterial walls can commence.

In infectious diseases caused by viruses, such as flu, herpes, and AIDS; or caused by bacteria, such as lung, inner ear, and bladder infections; lysine can stop or slow down an aggressive spread of infection. A combination of high dosages of vitamin C and other dietary supplements can bring additional benefits.

Even in the case of chronic inflammation of the stomach, intestines, joints, and bones the use of lysine can help keep the inflammation in check. Effective treatment of chronic inflammation involves the use of high dosages of lysine combined with other important dietary nutrients.

Even very common allergic problems, such as hay fever, neurodermatitis, or nettle rash, can benefit from the use of lysine, which can relieve the illness or prevent it. In these cases I also recommend combining lysine with vitamin C and other dietary supplements.

Use of Enzyme Blocks in Various Diseases

CANCER

ATHEROSCLEROSIS

INFECTIOUS DISEASES

- Viruses (flu, herpes, AIDS)
- Bacteria
  (lung, inner ear, bladder infections,)

CHRONIC INFLAMMATION

- Ulcers
- Intestinal inflammation
  (Colitis, Morbus Crohn)
- Arthritis
- Rheumatic disorders

ALLERGIC DISEASES

- Swollen blood vessels
  (angioedema)
- Nettle rash (urticaria)
- Skin diseases (neurodermatitis)
- Asthma (allergic asthma)
- Hay fever (allergic rhinitis)
- Conjunctivitis
  (inflammation of the eyes)

Please note: in the case of all these diseases, medical treatment is required. The recommendations in this book are not meant to replace consultation by a physician, only to supplement the medical treatment in a useful and natural way.

Conventional Cancer Therapy— a Dead-End Street

When you have reached this point in the book, you will undoubtedly ask yourself, "Is the medical world on the wrong track with its cancer therapy?" My answer would be, "Yes!"

The conventional treatment of cancer involves surgery, radiation therapy, and especially chemotherapy. None of these therapies has been proven to extend the life of a patient. This means that these therapies have been used for decades even though physicians know that it will not heal the disease and will often even accelerate it.

Constantly pressured by the pharmaceutical industry, patients are offered no options until they agree to chemotherapy. Chemotherapy means poisoning the cells. The pharmaceutical industry sells this cell poison with the argument that it will damage the cancer cells. What they do not tell patients is that all the other cells of the body are damaged as well. Thus chemo-poisoning of the bone marrow—the place where new blood cells are produced—will lead to anemia and increased susceptibility to infections. Chemo-poisoning of the mucous membrane cells of the gastrointestinal tract will lead to diarrhea and intestinal bleeding. The damage to hair follicles leads to extreme loss of hair.

Instead of strengthening the body's immune system to help fight the cancer, the chemotherapy will paralyze it. Chemotherapy's side effects require the additional use of other, new medications, such as antibiotics, plasma replacement drugs, painkillers,

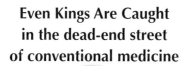

Even Kings Are Caught
in the dead-end street
of conventional medicine

King Hussein of Jordan † 1999
- The Victim of Chemotherapy -

cortisone, and many more. The last weeks or months of life for the patients undergoing cancer therapy are an Eldorado for the pharmaceutical industry.

It is not just ordinary people that end up in the dead-end street of conventional medicine, as we see in the example of King Hussein of Jordan. Convinced that he was receiving an excellent treatment for his leukemia (blood cancer), King Hussein moved to the Mayo Clinic in Rochester, MI. We all know the result: the chemotherapy destroyed the king's bone marrow. In order to replace it, a bone marrow transplant was required, which King Hussein did not survive. The chemotherapy killed the king faster than the actual disease would have.

Cancer—No Longer a Death Warrant

In 1992, I published the progress of Cellular Medicine™for the first time in a scientifically founded work called "Plasmin-induced proteolysis and the role of apopro-tein(a), lysine and synthetic lysine analogs". I asked Nobel laureate Linus Pauling to be my coauthor and to support the far-reaching results of my work.

For the first time in the history of medicine it was clear that:

- Not only cancer and some selected diseases, but also prac-tically all known diseases use the collagen-dissolving mechanism to spread through the body.
- The collagen-dissolving mechanism plays an important role in the formation of plaques in advanced atherosclerosis.
- The use of high-dosage lysine or lysine derivatives can slow down or halt the spread of almost every disease. The fact that lysine in combination with vitamin C can stabilize the connective tissue in the body is a medical breakthrough in the control of many diseases so far consi-dered incurable.
- The widespread use of this therapy will lead to a breakthrough in the fight against cancer, infectious diseases—including AIDS—and almost all other diseases.

The results of my study conclude that cancer diagnosis should no longer be a death warrant. As the following pages show, this research will also lead to a breakthrough in the treatment of AIDS.

Manuscript Page
of Dr. Rath's Scientific Publication

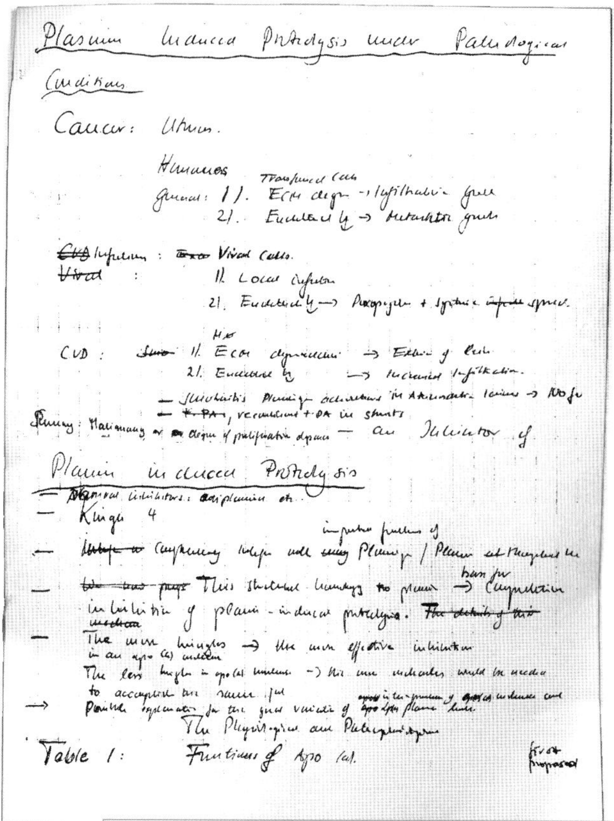
Plasmin induced Proteolysis under Pathological Conditions

Cancer: Tumors.

CVD:

Plasmin induced Proteolysis

— Kringle 4

Table 1: Functions of Apo (a).

Plasmin-Induced Proteolysis and the Role of Apoprotein(a), Lysine, and Synthetic Lysine Analogs

The most far-reaching consequence of my scientific research was the breakthrough in the fight against the AIDS epidemic. In the summary of my work I wrote, "It is foreseeable that the medical applications of lysine and synthetic lysine analogs, especially when combined with vitamin C, will lead to a breakthrough in the control of several forms of cancer, infectious diseases including AIDS, as well as many other diseases."

In 1992, when this work was published, the worldwide AIDS epidemic expanded to more than 10 million victims, and a successful AIDS therapy was not yet in sight. My discovery that this epidemic could be controlled by the use of lysine, a natural block of protein-digesting enzymes (proteases), was a breakthrough. Yet in the board rooms of the pharmaceutical companies it was ignored. In light of the fact that many medications were not thoroughly tested, it is no suprise that the AIDS epidemic largely contributed and still contributes to the profitable drug market.

At the same time, some therapeutic applications of my research have been explored. The employees of the pharmaceutical laboratories feverishly worked on synthetic, and therefore patented and profitable, protease blocks. In 1996 the breakthrough in the AIDS-therapy search was communicated with the first artificial protease-inhibitor introduced by the pharmaceutical companies.

Treatment with the new protease inhibitor will cost about $5,000 per patient per year. Millions of AIDS patients die in Africa, Asia, and South America because they cannot afford this medication.

15 Million AIDS Deaths
Were Avoidable

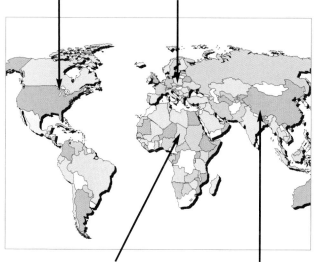

USA	Europe
Deaths: 1 Million	**Deaths:** 100.000
Patients: 2.5 Million	**Patients:** 680.000

Africa

Deaths: 12 Million
Patients: 22 Million

Asia

Deaths: 2 Million
Patients: 5 Million

World-Wide Toll for 1992:

Deaths: 15 Million People
Patients: 30 Million People

**The application of Cellular Health
can save millions of lives,
also in developing countries**

Notes

Principles of
Natural Therapies

- **Vitamin C and Lysine —**
  Key Molecules of Cellular Health

- **Collagen Production — A Key to**
  Disease Prevention and Control

- **Nutritional Supplementation with Proline,**
  Lysine, and Vitamin C

- **How Much Vitamin C —**
  The Tolerance Test

- **Cellular Health**

Vitamin C and Lysine: Key Molecules of Health

Cellular Health considers vitamin C (ascorbic acid) and the amino acid L-lysine as the most important natural substances. Their deficiency in humans can lead to dysfunction. There are two basic reasons why almost every person suffers from a deficiency of these cell factors: the human body cannot produce them, and our modern dietary habits cannot provide them in sufficient amounts. The result is that only marginal amounts of these substances are found in the body.

Almost all diseases thrive on a lack of vitamin C and lysine to spread through the body. This is related to the extraordinary value of these substances for the body's connective tissue. We can summarize this as follows:

1. Lysine inhibits the destruction of the connective tissue by preventing enzymatic digestion of collagen molecules. At the same time the amino acid lysine is a component of collagen and it is used for making the collagen in the body.

2. Vitamin C stimulates the production of the connective tissue and is essential for its optimal structure. Deficiency of vitamin C leads to tissue weakness and eventually to scurvy. On the other hand, an optimal supply of vitamin C assures optimal production of collagen and elastic fiber molecules and contributes to having strong connective tissue in the body.

Vitamin C and Lysine—
Effective Protection of the
Connective Tissue

Lysine
molecule

Cell

Collagen
molecule

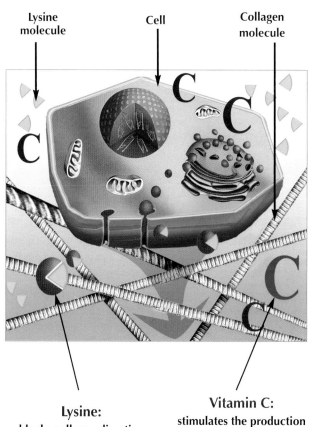

Lysine:
blocks collagen digesting
enzymes and disintegration
of the connective tissue

Vitamin C:
stimulates the production
of new collagen
and strengthens
connective tissue

Collagen Production — A Key to Disease Prevention and Control

Optimal production of collagen molecules is the precondition for control of aggressive diseases. The picture on the next page shows a muscle cell of the arterial wall. These arterial wall cells, among other physiological tasks, have to produce enough collagen molecules to maintain the arterial wall strong and elastic. For optimal collagen production they require three major nutrients:

- Vitamin C, which controls the collagen production from the cell nucleus's software. Collagen molecules, which wind around each other like a twilled rope, cannot attain theoptimal structure essential for biological activity and stability of collagen without the presence of vitamin C. This optimal biological conformation is attained when "chemical" bridges properly connect collagen strands, stabilizing the entire structure. These bridges are formed with oxygen and hydrogen atoms—the so-called "OH groups"—,which anchor specific lysine and proline molecules in collagen. This "hydroxylation" process is catalyzed by vitamin C.

- Lysine, which is a building block of the chain of amino acids that form collagen fibers. Since our body cannot produce its own lysine, every single lysine molecule must be supplied through the diet or from dietary supplements.

- Proline, which is another important amino acid component of collagen. Our body can produce it, but only in limited amounts. In people with long-term or aggressive diseases accompanied by the enzymatic destruction of tissue collagen, the body's capacity to produce proline can be exhausted. This often leads to a deficiency of this important amino acid.

Amino Acids Proline and Lysine Are Building Blocks of Collagen

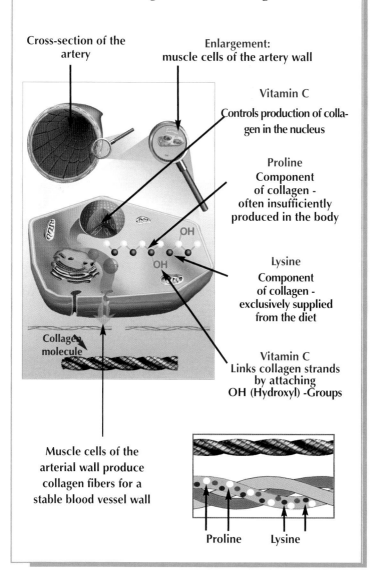

Cross-section of the artery

Enlargement: muscle cells of the artery wall

Vitamin C
Controls production of collagen in the nucleus

Proline
Component of collagen - often insufficiently produced in the body

Lysine
Component of collagen - exclusively supplied from the diet

Vitamin C
Links collagen strands by attaching OH (Hydroxyl) -Groups

Collagen molecule

Muscle cells of the arterial wall produce collagen fibers for a stable blood vessel wall

Proline   Lysine

61

Nutritional Supplementation
with Proline, Lysine and Vitamin C

Balanced quantities of L-proline, L-lysine, and vitamin C are essential for optimum production of collagen molecules. Lysine is an essential amino acid that has to be provided in our diet. Although proline can be synthesized in our body, its quantities may not be sufficient for specific body needs. An additional intake of proline can benefit people with an increased need for this amino acid.

Proline, Lysine and the "Principle of the Weakest Link"

Any system is only as good as its weakest part. This not only applies to a bucket filled with water, but also to the way our body produces collagen. Let me give you an example of a situation when proline is the weakest link in the collagen production chain. This would mean that this amino acid is the most needed. In such conditions collagen cannot be produced in optimum amounts even if the supply of lysine and vitamin C is sufficient. In this case, more proline must be provided. This is very important, because conventional medicine still erroneously believes that the body itself can produce any amount of proline and that an external supply is not needed. Following this wrong perception often brings fatal results.

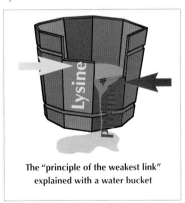

The "principle of the weakest link" explained with a water bucket

How Much Vitamin C Do I need?— A Tolerance Test

People very frequently ask me, "How much vitamin C do I need to take per day?" My answer is, "Only your own body can tell you this!" But what does this mean?

The daily vitamin C needs for your body to stay healthy depend on two basic factors: your genetic construction—the DNA (stretched cone)—and the actual health status of your body (short cone). As there is no system to measure the required daily need for vitamin C, we have to learn how to interpret the signals our body gives us. Too much vitamin C and the body will react with the signal of mild diarrhea. The reason: the excess vitamin C is excreted and causes fast bowels.

This method can only be used to measure an individual's need for vitamin C when following a step plan. Start taking the basic dietary supplement basic program and in addition take an extra amount of vitamin C, preferably in a complex form. Increase vitamin C intake gradually, by one gram a day, until you start to notice that your bowel movements become quicker. Now decrease the dosage by one or two grams and stay on it. This is your individual daily need of vitamin C.

California-based Dr. Cathcart established in his clinical research that patients with serious diseases could handle far higher amounts of vitamin C before they developed diarrhea than his healthy control group. Whereas in healthy people 8 to 10 grams a day were sufficient, patients with infections and other serious diseases could take 40 to 60 grams of vitamin C a day without problems—because of the body's increased need.

Cellular Health

Cellular Health emphasizes the importance of nutrient supplementation for optimum health. Vitamins, minerals, trace elements and amino acids are essential in optimizing cell function in the body. These nutrients blend together in cell metabolism like musicians like musicians in the orchestra.The requirements for particular nutrients vary from person to person and they largely depend on the genetic make-up, lifestyles or health conditions.

In general we need to make sure that nutrients such as vitamin C and amino acids lysine and proline are provided in optimum amounts. These nutrients are the building blocks of collagen, elastin and other components of the connective tissue in our body. They also include connective tissue-cementing elements, such as chondroitin sulfate and other glycosaminoglycans. These nutrients are essential for proper structure and optimal function of this tissue that builds and glues all cells together and forms body organs. These nutrients should be added to your diet gradually so your body has time to adjust and respond to them.

Today conventional medicine is in a stage of frustration. Despite millions of dollars spent on pharmacological research, cancer, coronary disease, and other common health problems keep spreading like wildfire. The only reason that these diseases are not controlled is that their true causes have not been understood or have been ignored; therefore no effective, conventional therapy is available.

Cellular Health - Paves the Way to the End of Common Diseases

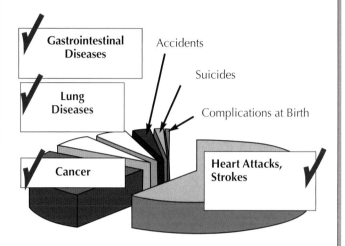

Gastrointestinal Diseases

Lung Diseases

Cancer

Accidents

Suicides

Complications at Birth

Heart Attacks, Strokes

The fourth-greatest cause of death: "Polypharmacy"

The above statistic by the World Health Organisation does not take into account that the serious side effects of medical drugs have now become the fourth-greatest cause of death, after heart infarction, cancer, and stroke. The pharmaceutical industry has even come up with a diagnostic term for this: "polypharmacy," meaning side effects from too much pharmaceutical medication.

The worldwide success of Cellular Health will now challenge "polypharmacy" - with a new, safe nutritional approach to many chronic diseases.

Questions and Answers

In this section, you can find answers to some of the questions you may have been asking yourself while reading the book.

Do vitamins and amino acids only help against the spreading of cancer or can they also help to prevent the development of cancer?

The development of cancer always proceeds through different stages. It starts with a cell that has been damaged by toxins from the diet, medication, radiation, or other damaging factors. In many cases the damaged cells die. Others survive and start to multiply uncontrollably. These cells are the cradles of the cancerous disease. Now only a weakness of the connective tissue is needed for the cells to multiply even more and start to spread, leading to cancer.

In all stages of the disease, including at the onset, vitamins have a protective function. Vitamin C, for instance, is decisive in the detoxification of the pharmaceutical drugs in the liver, which could otherwise lead to liver damage and liver cancer. Numerous studies have established that several other vitamins and substances have the same importance in cancer prevention. These include various antioxidants, such as carotenoids, vitamin E, co-enzyme Q10, among others.

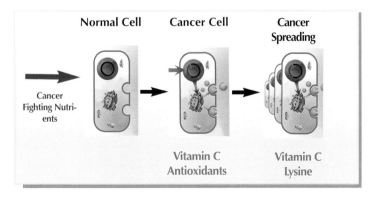

To prevent the cancer from spreading further, high dosages of lysine and vitamin C are particularly important, as I described in this book. That is why these natural substances are now available in a powdered form, so that the dosage can be easily increased when needed.

What about the government's recommended daily in-take (RDI)? Why are those lower than the ones you recommend in this book?

Advisory agencies on nutrition and the like have maintained for decades that 60 milligrams of vitamin C a day is sufficient to keep a person healthy. Generations of doctors have passed this false information on to their patients. Now the following has been established:

• There was or is no scientific or clinical research to substantiate these "recommendations."

• This small amount of vitamin C may be sufficient to prevent scurvy, but it can never guarantee the strength of the connective tissue that is needed to prevent the spread of disease.

• The consequence of this low vitamin C recommended dose is that many common diseases are still spreading among millions of people and creating a mass market for pharmaceutical products.

Exactly how do enzymes dissolve collagen?

In this book I have presented the mechanism of collagen digestion in a simplified way by using red "Pac-Man" characters. The actual process is somewhat more complex and is therefore summarised graphically on the next page. First, the cell secretes an enzyme, called the plasminogen-activator, which has the function of activating a second enzyme, called plasmin. Active plasmin then vitalizes a third enzyme, the pro-collagenase, and converts it to the final enzyme, collagenase. As we can deduce from the name, collagenase is the enzyme that digests the collagen, thus facilitating the conditions for cells to move around.

Is there a chance of side effects when taking nutrients in the dosages recommended in this book?

No. The vitamins, minerals, and amino acids that are not used up by the body cells are simply excreted. Remember that the human body has learned to deal with these natural substances for thousands of years. On the other hand, pharmaceutical products were developed in the test tubes of the pharmaceutical companies only this century. The human body treats them as foreign substances or cell toxins that have to be detoxified.

Naturally, "high" dosage is a relative term. Mammals—the goat for instance—can manufacture about 15 grams of vitamin C a day, and in cases of stress, even more. That is over 200 times the RDA "recommendation." Alternative cancer clinics in the United States treat patients with advanced stages of cancer with up to 200 grams of vitamin C a day—over 200,000 milligrams or 3,000 times the RDA recommendation. Naturally, these vitamin C doses must be given intravenously. However, it is a fact that to date no patient has died of an overdose of vitamin C, whereas hundreds of thousands die each year because they never hear about vitamin therapy to fight against serious disease, or they learn of it too late.

As has been discussed, no side effects or disruptions of normal body functions can be expected when taking lysine, even in dosages of several grams a day. However, the opposite is often the case. Many people die because this natural therapy is not applied.

Can every disease discussed in this book benefit from the Cellular Health approach?

Cellular Health is an important and natural way to help your body prevent and heal diseases. In many cases, however—especially in the advanced stages of a disease—Cellular Health cannot fully recover your health. Extensive research is being done to try and make these cases the exceptions.

Scientific Details of Enzymatic Collagen Digestion and Lysine Blocking

Blocking by Lysine

Plasminogen-Activator

1. Enzyme

Plasmin

2. Enzyme

Pro-collagenase

3. Enzyme

Collagenase

4. Enzyme

The following bibliography contains important studies on blocking collagen degradation as well as on the use of vitamins to combat cancer and other diseases.

Literature and Sources

Almer, S., Andersson, T., Strom, M. (1992) Pharmacokinetics of tranexamic acid in patients with ulcerative colitis and in healthy volunteers after the single instillation of 2 g rectally. Journal of Clinical Pharmacology 32: 49-54.

Astedt, B., Glifberg, I., Mattson, W., et al. (1977) Arrest of growth of ovarian tumour by tranexamic acid. Journal of the American Medical Association 238: 154-155.

Astedt, B., Mattson, W., Trope, C. (1977) Treatment of advanced breast cancer with chemotherapeutics and inhibition of coagulation and fibrinolysis. Acta Medica Scandinavica 201: 491-493.

Block, G. (1991) Dietary guidelines and the results of food consumption surveys. American Journal of Clinical Nutrition 53(1): 356S-357S.

Block, G. (1991) Epidemiological evidence regarding vitamin C and cancer. American Journal of Clinical Nutrition 32(6): 1310S-1314S.

Block, G. (1991) Vitamin C and cancer prevention: the epidemiological evidence (see comments). American Journal of Clinical Nutrition 53(1): 270S-282S.

Block, G. (1992) Vitamin C status and cancer. Epidemiological evidence of reduced risk. Annals of the New York Academy of Sciences 53(AD): 280-90.

Blohm,È, G. (1972) Treatment of hereditary angioneurotic oedema with tranexamic acid. Acta Medica Scandinavica 192: 293-298.

Bramsen, T. (1977) Effect of tranexamic acid on choroidal melanoma. Acta Ophthalmologica 56: 264-269.

Buckley. D.I., McPherson, R.S., North, C.Q., et al. (1992) Dietary micronutrients and cervical dysplasia in southwestern American Indian women. Nutrition and Cancer 61(2): 179-85.

Cathcart, R.F. (1991) A unique function for ascorbate. Medical Hypotheses 35: 32-37.

Daviglus, M.L., Dyer, A.R., Persky, V., et al. (1996) Dietary beta-carotene, vitamin C, and risk of prostate cancer: results from the Western Eclectic Study (see comments). Epidemiology 32(5): 472-7.

Flagg, E.W., Coates, R.J., Greenberg, R.S. (1995) Epidemiological studies of antioxidants and cancer in humans. Journal of the American College of Nutrition 32(5): 419-27.

Gaby, S.K., Bendich, A., Singh, V.N., et al. (1991) Vitamin intake and health. Marcell Dekker, Inc., N.Y., N.Y.

Hansen, P.H., Rasmussen, L.B. (1982) Progressiv demens. Ugeskr LÊger 144/31: 2289-2290.

Hardy, J.F., BÈlisle, S., Dupont, C., et al. (1998) Prophylactic tranexamic acid and epsilon-aminocaproic acid for primary myocardial revascularisation. Ann Thorac Surg 65(2): 371-6.

Henson, D., Block, G., Levine, M., (1991) Ascorbic acid: biological functions and relation to cancer. Journal of the National Cancer Institute 83/8: 547-550.

Hollanders, D., Thomson, J.M., Schofield, P.F. (1982) Tranexamic acid therapy in ulcerative colitis. Postgraduate Medical Journal 58: 87-91.

Kohga, S., Harvey, S.R., Weaver, R.M., et al. (1985) Localisation of plasminogen activators in human colon cancer by immunoperoxidase staining. Cancer Research 45: 1787-1796.

Kwaan, H.C., Astrup, T. (1964) Fibrinolytic activity of reparative connective tissue. Journal of Pathology and Bacteriology 87: 409.

Larsson, G., Larsson, A., Astedt, B. (1987) Tissue plasminogen activator and urokinase in normal, dysplastic and cancerous squamous epithelium of the uterine cervix. Thrombosis and Haemostasis 58(3): 822-826.

Laurberg, G. (1977) Tranexamic acid in chronic urticaria: a double-blind study. Acta Dermatovener (Stockholm) 57: 369-370.

Maramag, C., Menon, M., Balaji, K.C., et al. (1997) Effect of vitamin C on prostate cancer cells in vitro: effect on cell number, viability, and DNA synthesis. Prostate 32(3): 188-95.

Maramag, C., Menon, M., Balaji, K.C., et al. (1997) Reduced mononuclear leukocyte ascorbic acid content in adults with insulin-dependent diabetes mellitus consuming adequate dietary vitamin C. Metabolism 32(3): 146-9.

Marasini, B., Cicardi, G.C., Martignoni, G.C., et al. (1978) Treatment of hereditary angioedema. Klinische Wochenschrift 56: 819-823.

Marcus, S.L., Dutcher, J.P., Paietta, E., et al. (1987) Severe hypovitaminosis C occurring as the result of adoptive immunotherapy with high-dose interleukin 2 and lymphokine-activated killer cells. Cancer Research 47: 4208-4212.

Martens, B.P.M. (1984) Clinical experience with tranexamic acid in urticaria and angioedema. British Journal of Dermatology 111: 481-482.

Munch, E.P., Weeke, B. (1985) Non-hereditary angioedema treated with tranexamic acid. Allergy 40: 92-97.

Ngkeekwong, F.C. (1997) Two distinct uptake mechanisms for ascorbate and dehydroascorbate in human lymphoblasts and their interaction with glucose. Biochemical Journal 76(3): 225-30.

Ocke, M.C., Kromhout, D., Menotti, A., et al. (1997) Vitamin C inhibits random migration of malignant pleural effusion mononuclear cells. Archivum immunologiae et therapiae experimentalis (Warszawa) 61(4): 87-91.

Paganelli, G.M., Biasco, G., Brandi, G. (1992) Effect of vitamin A, C and E supplementation on rectal cell proliferation in patients with colorectal adenomas. Journal of the National Cancer Institute 32(1): 47-51.

Pandey, D.K., Shekelle, R., Selwyn, B.J., et al. (1995) Dietary vitamin C and beta-carotene and risk of death in middle-aged men. The Western Eclectic Study. American Journal of Epidemiology 65(12): 1269-78.

Poydock, M.E. (1991) Effect of combined ascorbic acid and B-12 on survival of mice with implanted Ehrlich carcinoma and L1210 leukemia. American Journal of Clinical Nutrition 76(3): 1261S-1265S.

Rath, M. (1991) Solution to the puzzle of human cardiovascular disease: its primary role is ascorbate deficiency, leading to the deposition of lipoprotein(a) and fibrinogen/fibrin in the vascular wall. Journal of Orthomolecular Medicine 7: 17-23.

Rath, M. (1992) Plasmin induced proteolysis and the role of apoprotein(a), lysine and synthetic lysine analogs. Journal of Orthomolecular Medicine 7: 17-23.

Rath, M. (2001) Cellular Health Series: The Heart. MR Publihing Inc., Santa Clara, CA.

Rivas, C.I., Vera, J.C., Guaiquil, V.H., et al. (1997) Increased uptake and accumulation of vitamin C in human immunodeficiency virus 1-infected hematopoietic cell lines. Journal of Biological Chemistry 272(9): 5814-20.

Roomi, M.W., House, D., Eckert-Macksic, M., et al. (1998) Growth suppression of malignant leukemia cell line in vitro by ascorbic acid (vitamin C) and its derivatives. Cancer Letters 122(1-2): 93-9.

Sheffer, A.L., Austen, K.F., Rosen, F.S. (1972) Tranexamic acid therapy in hereditary angioneurotic oedema. New England Journal of Medicine 287: 452-454.

Sigurdsson, K., Johnsson, J.E., Trope, C. (1983) Tranexamic acid for the treatment of advanced ovarian carcinoma. Acta obstetriticia et gynecologica scandinavica 62: 265-266.

Skriver, L., Larsson, L.I., Kielberg, V., et al. (1984) Immuno-cytochemical localisation of urokinase-type plasminogen activator in Lewis lung carcinoma. Journal of Cell Biology 99: 752-757.

Smith, M.E., Amaducci, L.A. (1982) Observations on the effects of protease inhibitors on the suppression of experimental allergic encephalomyelitis. Neurochemical Research 7/5: 541-554.

Some, H., Sashida, T., Yosida, M., et al. (1980) Treatment of advanced ovarian cancer with fibrinolytic inhibitor (tranexamic acid). Acta obstetrica et gynecologica scandinavica 59: 285-287.

Strickland, S., Beers, W.H. (1976) Studies on the role of plasminogen activator in ovulation. Journal of Biological Chemistry 251/18: 5694-5702.

VanEenwyk, J., Davis, F.G., Colman, N. (1992) Folate, vitamin C, and cervical intraepithelial neoplasia (see comments). Cancer Epidemiology, Biomarkers and Prevention 61(2): 119-24.

Werb, Z., Mainardi, C.L., Vater, C.A., et al. (1977) Endegenous activation of latent collagenase by rheumatoid synovial cells. New England Journal of Medicine 296/18.

Zhang, H.M., Wakisaka, N., Maeda, O., et al. (1997) Vitamin C inhibits the growth of a bacterial risk factor for gastric carcinoma: Helicobacter pylori. Cancer 32(10): 1897-903.